Rose

A Play

Andrew Davies

Samuel French – London
New York – Sydney – Toronto – Hollywood

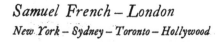

FOR AMATEUR PRODUCTION ENQUIRIES

UNITED KINGDOM AND WORLD EXCLUDING NORTH AMERICA
plays@samuelfrench.co.uk
020 7255 4302/01

Each title is subject to availability from Samuel French, depending upon country of performance.

ROSE

First produced by Colin Brough at the Duke of York's Theatre, London, on the 28th February 1980, with the following cast of characters:

Rose	Glenda Jackson
Mother	Jean Heywood
Smale	Stephanie Cole
Malpass	Gillian Martell
Jim Beam	Tom Georgeson
Sally	Diana Davies
Jake	Richard Vanstone
Geoffrey	David Daker
Father	Richard Vanstone

The play directed by ALAN DOSSOR
Settings by John Gunter

The action takes place in and around a Midlands town

Time—the present

NOTE ON THE SETTING

On each side of the stage are four doors, painted black in a black wall. Across the back wall are three arched entrances, also black, which can be covered by black curtains. No front-stage lighting is directed on these entrances, and the floor in front of them is also painted black. The main acting area is a brightly lit square c. Furniture and properties for the various scenes are brought on and off by the stage management during the action, so that it flows without a break.

ACT I

Slops Wine Bar

The Light comes up on Rose, seated at a table in the Bar. There is a half-pint of bitter for Rose and a sherry for her mother on the table

> *Smale, Malpass, Beam, Mother, Sally, Geoffrey and Jake each open a door and stand in the doorway with the Lights behind them as their voices surround Rose*

Smale Mrs Malpass will tell the story. Fingers on lips.

Malpass Once upon a time there was a little girl who thought she was very clever.

Beam I'm just looking for some kind of spark, you know? I think you might have got it.

Mother You must be fond of a treat, turning out on a night like this.

Sally Warwickshire's a lovely county, Rose, it's just the people who live here.

Geoffrey Do you know, there's not so much as a piece of bloody cheese in the fridge.

Jake Susan.

Geoffrey It doesn't matter.

Jake No, Rose.

The sound of children's voices is heard

Smale Is that your class, Mrs Fidgett?

Malpass She just sails through it.

Sally Don't you let 'em get you.

Malpass She seems to think it's fun.

Geoffrey You care for nothing and you notice bloody nothing.

The sound increases

Smale One line. With your partners. Now don't you dare move. That's better.

The sound fades, the doors close and the Lights change

> *Mother comes in and sits with Rose*

Mother Well, that was a nasty experience, Rose. And the lock wouldn't work.

Rose Did you get invaded then?

Mother I'd like to see them try.

Rose Well never mind, you'll be all right at the theatre, Mother, they've got quite a nice one there.

Mother I'll beg leave to doubt *that*, Rose. Seemed a pokey little place to me. And that lad in the ticket office. Selling tickets in his vest, there's no need for that!

Rose Well, it's only the *studio* theatre, Mother.

Mother They used to do that in evening suits. That lad at the ballet had one.

Rose Who?

Mother That time you took me to the ballet.

Rose Which time?

Mother That time we went to the ballet. The *only* time! When we went to the *big* theatre, the *proper* theatre! Don't you remember, Rose, we were sat there, waiting, and then a man came on in evening dress with a piece of paper . . .

Rose Oh, yes.

Mother And then he said that owing to an indisposition Serge somebody would not be able to dance the part of the Prince, and everyone in the whole theatre moaned. Yes, a great moan went up. It's funny, I didn't know who this Serge was from Adam, I'd never seen him in my life before, but I felt I had to join in that moan. (*Pause*) I enjoyed that moment more than anything else in the whole evening.

Rose You would.

Mother (*sharply*) What?

Rose Nothing.

Mother You didn't have to ask me out tonight, you know.

Rose I *wanted* to.

Mother Can't think why.

Rose Oh, Mother.

Pause

Mother That's the only evening suit I've set eyes on all the time I've been down here.

Rose Well, they don't wear them so much nowadays.

Mother You don't need to tell me that, Rose, that's what I'm saying. No danger of finding one in this place, is there? What do they call it?

Rose Slops Wine Bar, Mother.

Mother Yes. I know what sort of place this is.

Rose What?

Mother (*with deep contempt*) Casual.

Rose Oh, dear.

Mother There's no need to make fun of me, Rose, you know what I'm talking about. Look at that one behind the bar, I'd like to know what *his* aim is, shirt open down to there. And ear-rings. *That's* not necessary, Rose.

Rose He's only got one ear-ring, Mother.

Mother Don't know what he's so proud of, he's as hairy as a monkey.

Rose Mother!

Mother And he's got a belly like a poisoned pup.

Rose Ssh!

Mother No need to shush me, they don't care one way or the other, people like that.

Rose Oh, Mother, how d'you *know*?

Mother Well, it's obvious, Rose.

Rose Oh, that's typical.

Mother I didn't ask to come here tonight, I know you didn't want to bring me.

Rose I did, I did, look how many times I asked you.

Mother Oh, asking's one thing.

Rose What's that supposed to mean?

Mother I don't want to say any more about it.

Rose I wanted you to come out with me, I wanted you to come out with me and have a nice time. I thought we'd enjoy ourselves! I thought it would be nice for you to come out and see somewhere different and have a couple of drinks, instead of being stuck home every night!

Mother There's no need for you to feel sorry for me.

Rose (*loudly*) It's not that!

Mother Ssh!

Rose It's not that! Can't you understand it? I thought it would be nice to go out with you for a change!

They are both cross with each other

Mother What's the matter with your husband?

Rose There's nothing the matter with my husband! I wish you wouldn't call him that.

Mother Well, he is that, isn't he?

Rose He's got a name.

Mother I know he's got a name, there's no need to talk to me as if I was half-witted, and where is he anyway?

Rose It doesn't matter where he is, he's got nothing to do with this, this was going to be an evening for you and me.

Mother Hm.

Rose He's got some thing on in Birmingham.

Mother What sort of thing?

Rose I don't know. One of his things.

Mother Well, hope he remembers he's married.

Mother brings this out with some triumph. Rose lets out a big exasperated sigh. Pause. Then she makes an effort

Rose Mother! Look. Let's have another drink. We've got time.

Mother No, thank you.

Rose Oh, come on.

Mother Nor for me, Rose, thank you.

Rose I think I will.

Mother I don't need alcohol to enjoy myself. It's no use trying to turn me into an alcoholic.

Rose I'm not trying to turn you into an alcoholic, I just thought you might fancy the other half, that's all!

Mother And I don't like to see women drinking beer either.

Rose I'll turn the other way.

Mother I'm sorry, I just don't like to see it. Women never used to drink beer.

Rose Ah, well, that's emancipation for you, Mother. But I only drink halves, don't I? Only halfway there in the struggle for self-realization. The spirit's willing, honest, it's just the flesh. If it weren't for the dreaded cystitis, I'd drink pint for pint with any man here.

Mother No need for that, Rose.

Rose Oh, think of all the things there's no *need* for! If we were all like you no-one would ever do *anything*!

Mother Well, I'm sorry I'm spoiling your evening, I can see you won't invite me again in a hurry.

Rose Look, for the last time, I *wanted* you to come with me, and I'm sorry if I *asked* and *asked*, but *I don't know* any other way of getting people to do things.

There is a splutter of protest from Mother

What did you want me to do, kidnap you? And I just wish you'd stop talking about spoiling my evening and no need for this and no need for that, because I wish you could just get it into your *thick* head that this is supposed to be *fun*, you and me going out together and having a nice time just for a change, because you're my *mother* and I *love* you!

Mother If you're going to talk to me like that I'm going now.

Rose Like what, for Christ's sake? What do you *want*?

Mother Somebody here might know us!

Rose Nobody here knows us! Nobody knows anybody!

Mother Oh, stop trying to be clever, you don't suit it. All right, if you're quite determined that I've got to make an exhibition of myself, I'll tell you! I don't want you worrying about me and feeling guilty about me, and I know it's not for me anyway, it's to make you feel better; and if you think I'm not making an effort and keeping my mind alive, well, haven't you ever stopped to think I might not *want* to keep my mind alive? What do I want to keep my mind alive for? I don't need to keep my mind alive! You're like that woman next door always trying to get me to go and play Bingo with her!

Rose Well, why not Bingo?

Mother I'll tell you why not Bingo, because I did go once, which you never have, I went with that woman next door, and we sat and played Bingo, all us old widows, and it might have been all right for them, but it wasn't all right for me, he didn't even say Kelly's eye and two fat ladies or whatever it is, it was just the numbers, no pretending there was any fun about it at all, just a lot of old widows trying to take their minds off waiting to die, seventy-nine, eighty-five, all those numbers, it just makes it worse, if you had the wit to see it, but you don't, you just think about yourself, don't you, and whether you've done enough, well you have, you've done quite enough, and you don't have to worry about me any more, thank you very much, and it was very nice of you to take me out, but you needn't have bothered. You'll see when you come to it yourself, it'll be like the scales falling off your eyes, you'll see. You just want to be let alone, and not mucked about, and made to see the point of things. Ooh, it'll be such a relief when I'm dead. Eeh! I'm sorry about that little outburst, I think I'll take meself home now, you go to the play and enjoy yourself, Rose . . .

Rose Don't be silly. I'll come with you.

Mother No, I'd never forgive myself.

Rose Right!

Mother No, I'll get the bus and I'll be home and tucked up in bed by nine and that'll have seen another day off, it's putting the time in that counts. *(She suddenly stands up, produces a pound note and slaps it down)* Have one for me. *(She walks off)*

Rose Mother!

Mother And remember you're married!

Mother goes

Rose Terrible. Terrible.

Rose gets up, comes forward and addresses the audience. During the following, the scene is set for Assembly

Well, I'm sorry to have inflicted all that on you. I mean I do realize that you can perfectly well get all that sort of thing in your own homes, I mean you've all got mothers somewhere, I s'pose. Yes? And my only excuse is this, something Rosa Luxembourg said: that it's in the tiny domestic struggles of individual people as they grope towards self-realization that we can most truly discern the great movements of society. Splendid, that. I wonder where I got it. Back of a matchbox, perhaps. Must have been a bloody big matchbox. Household size? Look, I can see you're worrying about mother, but it's *all right*. She did catch the bus, just like she said she would, and no one molested her, in fact she had a very nice chat with a Sikh conductor about the manners of the younger generation. And I tore myself away from the delights of Slop's Wine Bar and took myself and two tickets to the theatre. *(To scene shifters)* Thank you. *(Turning back to the audience) And* I went round next day, *and* we made it up, no hard feelings, because she is my mother, and I do love her and who else has she got, and we have that sort of scene, if you can believe it, about once every three weeks; and really, if her idea of enjoying herself is having a bad time, who am I to interfere in the twilight of her life? Still you know all about that. And anyway, this isn't about her, it's about me, she thinks it's about her but it isn't, it's about me. I'm not just a pretty face. I have a job. I teach six-year-olds in an infant school, and it's worthwhile, and I'm quite ambitious, I fancy becoming some new kind of headmistress eventually, but ooh, I don't know. If you could see it. Let's say it's assembly, and I'm late.

Malpass and Smale come on. Malpass sits at the piano, playing, and Smale stands facing the "children"—the audience

Smale	*(singing lustily together)*	Jesus loves me, this I know
Malpass		For the Bible tells me so

Little ones to him belong
They are weak but he is strong.

Rose sneaks on

Yes, Jesus loves me
Yes, Jesus loves me

Rose joins in

All (*singing*)   Yes, Jesus loves me
The Bible tells me so.

Smale has noticed Rose's late arrival with disapproval. Smale's fierce eyes are everywhere, glaring at imaginary offenders in the audience

Smale And now, let me see you all sitting very quietly. Fingers on lips. I'm waiting, Garth. *Fingers on lips.* Thank you. Now Mrs Malpass will tell the story, and today the story is called "The Wonderful Box".

Smale and Rose sit down, Malpass steps forward

Malpass Once upon a time there was a little girl called Jane; and she went to school, just like you, but she wasn't a very happy little girl. Because she was very poor, and she didn't have any toys to play with. Every day she'd see the other children playing with their toys: the boys with their footballs and the girls with their dolls . . .

Rose winces

But oh, how Jane wished that she had something of her very own to play with. It was no use asking her mother, because she knew her mother didn't have any money to spare. So she became sadder and sadder. Then one morning, as she was walking to school, suddenly she noticed something in the gutter. What d'you think it was?

Smale leans forward urgently, fingers on lips, lest someone break the silence

It was a little wooden box. It was shiny and carved, with a little golden lock with the key in it, and Jane thought she'd never seen such a beautiful box. She bent down—(*she mimes it*)—and she turned it round in her hands—and then she turned the key and opened the lid—and what a surprise! Beautiful music came out of the box! It was a musical box! And then she closed the box, and hugged it tight. But then she thought: It's not my box. So she stood there, clutching the box and wondering what to do. And what d'you think she did?

Smale leans forward as before

No! She was a good, honest little girl, although she was so poor, and she did take it to her teacher. And the teacher went with her to the police station, and the policeman said he was very sorry, but a rich little boy had come to the police station in a big shiny car and said he'd lost the box. It belonged to him.

Rose blows out a great breath

So you can imagine how sad Jane was. But the very next day, the same big shiny car drew up outside Jane's house, and out of it got the rich little boy and his daddy, and the daddy had a parcel in his hand. Another box! Almost as beautiful as the one Jane had found. "Open it," said the rich little boy. And very slowly Jane opened it. (*She mimes*) And the box played a beautiful tune for Jane. Can you hear the music? I can hear it. (*She cups her hand to her ear*) Cup your hands to your ears when I open the box. (*She opens it*)

Smale, glaring, and Rose, deadpan, cup their hands to their ears simultaneously like a backing group

And then the rich little boy and his daddy got into the big shiny car and drove away. But Jane was very happy, because she had something of her own to play with at last! And it was all because she was a *good, honest* little girl who respected other people's property. And if you are all good honest boys and girls—I'm sure you are—who knows? Maybe one day you might have a wonderful box of your own.

With a demure, smug, almost embryonic curtsey to Smale, Malpass sits down

Smale Stand up. Hands together. Close eyes. *Tight. Everybody.* Mrs Fidgett will say the prayer for today.

Rose is alarmed, she had forgotten it was her turn. She will have to improvize

Rose Oh God.

A rather long pause. Rose's mind has gone blank. Smale and Malpass go very tense. Rose clears her throat

Oh God. Help us to make this a happy day at school. Help us to enjoy the maths and the work cards and the apparatus and the music and movement today. Look after us at play time and help us not to get into fights with each other. You know we sometimes have to get into fights, but most of them are silly and just hurt us and other people. Oh God, it would be very good if you could help us to get through today without kicking anyone or sptting at anyone, or crying . . . or losing our tempers, or hurting anyone's feelings, or being very boring. (*Pause. She cannot think of anything else to say*) Amen.

Smale
Malpass } (*together*) { Amen.

Rose sits down and Smale gives her an old-fashioned look

Smale One more thing. Some boys in this school—have been doing some very bad things. They know who they are. And I know who they are. Yes. I am talking about the boys' toilets. Now some of us here are not yet five years old, and some of us are nearly seven, but I think we all know how we should behave in the toilets. I am not pleased about this, and you know what that means, don't you? Oh, I know who it is all right. Some silly, dirty, nasty little boys. They know who they are, and they know I know. And they will come and tell me about it, because they know they will not be forgiven unless they do. Well, we won't say any more about it now. The silly, dirty, nasty little boys will come to my room, and the rest of you will be very very careful about what you do in the toilets. That's all. Lead out quietly.

Malpass exits

Rose steps forward and the stage is cleared except for Rose's and Smale's chairs

Rose That's it. It doesn't really take very long, but the idea is to set the tone for the day. It's a traditional assembly, as these things go. You know: hymn, prayer, story, bollocking. I mean, some of the sentiments are wholesome. Be good, be honest, don't pee on the wall—but there's got to be more to it than that.

Smale Mrs Fidgett!

Rose Yes, Mrs Smale.

Smale Could I have a word, Mrs Fidgett?

Rose Yes, of course, Mrs Smale. It's Ms Strong, if you remember. Sorry.

Smale Oh, yes. It is rather confusing, changing your name like that, er, Ms Strong. Don't you find it confuses the children?

Rose Well, I did explain it to them, Mrs Smale and they thought it was quite a good idea. Well, it was my name first. Before I married Mr Fidgett.

Smale Yes, you did explain it to me.

Rose And who'd be a Fidgett when they could be Strong? No, well, my husband said a Rose by any other name would smell as sweet, which was quite apt and poetic for him, but still. . . . It is a point of principle with me.

Smale We have been through all this.

Rose Yes, sorry. It's just that no-one seems to remember. Sorry. Not you. I know you have a lot to remember.

Smale Yes. While we are on points of principle, could I ask you whether it's a point of principle with you to depart from the prayers in the book, as you did this morning?

Rose No! Not really, Mrs Smale, what it really was, was, I forgot it was my turn this morning and I forgot the book, so I just—extemporized.

Smale Did you.

Rose Didn't you like it then?

Smale (*slightly thrown*) That's not really the point, Mrs—Ms Strong. I have the parents to contend with. And the Office.

Rose Oh, yes, the Office.

Smale I think it's best if we keep to the pattern in the book, don't you? (*Turning as she goes*) I see you've put in for one or two deputy head's posts?

Rose Oh, I didn't realize you'd . . .

Smale I've had two requests for confidential reports.

Rose Oh, yes. Well, yes. Thought I'd have a go. You know.

Smale Thought you'd have a go.

Rose That's it. You know.

Smale No, I'm not sure that I do know.

Rose Well, I have got quite a lot of experience now—

Smale As a classroom teacher, yes?

Rose —and I've actually got quite a few ideas I thought we might—(*she hesitates*) Well, when you have the time—maybe I'd better—

Smale Oh, yes? (*She waits*)

Rose I mean—well, for example, I'd like to involve the parents a whole lot more, let them come in when they like and get stuck in with the kids if they want to. I know what some of the parents are like but, they wouldn't necessarily be the ones who . . .

Smale And of course you'd be happy to take full responsibility for admitting some and excluding others, and handling any complaints to the education office . . .

Rose Yes, I s'pose there would be difficulties, but it would be worth it to get a few fathers into the school. It's really sinister the way you hardly ever see a man in an infant school.

Smale Sinister?

Less sure of herself, Rose struggles on, recovering as she goes

Rose No, well—I suppose what it all boils down to is I'd like schools to be places where people have a lot of fun and excitement, the kids and the teachers, instead of going round all scared and miserable and wondering what we've done wrong *now*. (*She has gone too far*) Ah. I, er, didn't mean to be rude, I know it must seem as if I'm knocking the way you do things. I s'pose we all see things our own way. (*Pause*) Oh, dear. Look, I'm sorry. I got carried away.

Smale Mrs—Ms Strong. Won't you sit down?

Rose Thank you.

Smale This school is in a very difficult area, and yet it enjoys a very high reputation. Whatever you happen to think of it.

Rose Yes, I know, Mrs Smale.

Smale When I took it over, ten years ago, it was a sink.

Rose A sink.

Smale I could use other words. The children were like dirty little wild animals. The staff were totally demoralized. The director of education took me aside. Your task, Mrs Smale, he said, is to cleanse the Augean stables. And that is what I have done. Now it's a school that parents are proud to send their children to.

Rose Yes, I know they are, Mrs Smale, I didn't mean . . .

Smale It can even accommodate the occasional eccentric, Ms Strong, without having its values too seriously undermined.

Pause

Rose I don't just—undermine your values, Mrs Smale.

Smale I know that. You're a talented classroom teacher; I think that you have a good deal of flair.

Rose (*taken aback, flattered*) Oh.
Smale I think that's where you might make your most valuable contribution, don't you?
Rose It's not that I want to get away from class teaching . . .
Smale I'm glad to hear that. And I'm pleased that you're beginning to take an interest in the wider issues involved in running a school, of this kind. Ms Strong—I'll be very happy to discuss them with you when you've had a little more time to sort out your ideas. (*Briskly: Rose disposed of*) Well, work to do, work to do.

Smale bustles off, taking her chair

During the following, the Staffroom scene is set and then Smale and Malpass come in

Rose I think I handled that really well, don't you? Hm. She doesn't think I could do it. Christ, you don't *have* to be like that to run a school, do you? Never come across a head teacher like me, though. Rose, head teacher. Seems to be a bit of a credibility gap there. Oh, come on. She was just narked with me. Course, my big mistake was mentioning fun and excitement; that doesn't half put people into a rage these days. I might as well have used a rude word. Well, Mrs Smale, I feel that schools should be places where people can have a lot of bollocks and balls, don't you feel that? No, they don't feel that. I mean, take the other day in the staffroom, peaceful enough scene, kettle burbling gently on the hob.

Rose goes, taking her chair

Malpass is sitting in one of the armchairs with Smale standing behind her, massaging her neck and shoulders with affectionate expertise

Rose comes in, sits on the small chair, opens "The Guardian" and reads it, glancing across now and then. From her reactions it can be gathered that this massage scene is not unusual

Malpass Oh, yes, I think it's easing.
Smale Best not to talk, Beryl. Just try to relax.
Rose Headache again?
Smale (*severely*) Migraine.
Rose Oh. Rotten luck.
Malpass You're so good at it, Mrs Smale. Much better than my husband. Really.
Smale It's a knack.
Malpass No, it's more than that. I've tried to show him so many times, and really he'd *like* to help, but he's no use at all.
Smale Well, I think that's often the way.
Malpass It's as if he's got no imagination in his fingers, as if he can't feel anything through them. Oh, yes, that's it again. There.
Smale Ssh.
Malpass And then again, I think he gets bored.
Smale Well, men. They haven't got the patience. (*The kettle has boiled and*

she goes and makes two cups of coffee) What do you say, Mrs—Ms—Rose?

Rose Some have, some haven't I suppose.

Smale thinks "obstinate cow" and shows it

No, well, I must admit, in my limited experience, you're quite right.

Malpass You can't expect it of them.

Rose Why not?

Malpass (*trying to formulate*) Well—you just wouldn't. It's not—well, it doesn't seem to be in their natures.

Smale Steady, Beryl. Don't let yourself tense up.

Rose Look, don't take any notice of me, I'll just read the paper.

Malpass It was that six o'clock news bulletin last night that started it off. I got so tensed up with it, I could feel my head just starting to throb.

Rose What was it?

Malpass That case.

Rose Oh yes.

Smale hands Rose a mug of coffee

(*To Smale*) Thank you.

Malpass You know. I think I'm a broadminded person. I don't think I'm easily shocked—

Smale hands Malpass a mug of coffee

(*To Smale*) thank you—but to think of putting all those details on television.

Smale (*between her teeth*) Yes. (*She resumes the massage*)

Rose Yes, it was a bit squirmy. Must be awful, having your private life splurged all over the box. Seen from the outside. Must feel terrible.

Malpass I wasn't thinking about him, I was thinking about the children *watching it.*.On *television.*

Smale Yes.

Rose But they didn't show anything, did they? I thought they were just talking about it.

Malpass Don't you think that's enough? At six o'clock?

Rose What?

Smale *Homosexuality.*

Malpass And we're supposed to educate children in an atmosphere like that.

Malpass stiffens at the word, then closes her eyes. Smale glares at Rose then returns her full attention to the massage. Rose watches as Malpass gradually relaxes again. It's a peaceful little scene, but she cannot leave it alone

Rose (*gently*) But—don't you think, in a way, it's quite good for children to hear about these things, at home, you know, and you can explain things to them.

Malpass How could I explain a thing like that to my daughter? She's never heard of *such* a thing.

Smale (*between her teeth*) Well, of course she hasn't.

Malpass You've got to protect them, haven't you?

Smale Quite. It becomes more difficult day by day. I can ensure that they're not—damaged by anything like that when they're in my school, but I don't know how people expect us to teach them about—love—in a proper atmosphere when as soon as they go home they're exposed to—that.

Malpass Yes.

Pause

Rose (*gently*) But even so—I mean, it's just a kind of love. What if they love each other? That's not so awful, is it? You don't have to think about what they do if it upsets you, I mean sex is mostly emotion and feelings and that, isn't it?

Smale Not for men.

Rose Well, I dunno. Maybe not so much. But honestly, it's ever so common.

Smale One in ten, I've read. But I can't credit that.

Malpass Oh, I can. There's so much about it on television and in the papers, if people didn't hear so much about it they wouldn't have it on their minds. And some people are silly enough to do anything if they think it's in the fashion.

Rose Oh, Beryl, you're a marvel, you make it sound like wedge heels! (*Getting carried away by her idea*) Blimey, you don't read about it in the paper and say, oh, long evening skirts are out but dykes are in, I'd better rush down the Precinct and get one before they all go!

Smale I don't know what you're talking about.

It would be politic for Rose to shut up: she tries, but she cannot

Rose Homosexuality! It's not a fashion, it's how you're born and brought up, and anyway we're none of us a hundred per cent one thing or the other!

Smale Please! There's no need.

Rose I'm sorry, sorry, Beryl. It's just—I mean one in ten, well take the children in this school. What is it, thirty-five kids to a class, chances are some of them'll grow up gay.

Malpass You're talking about six-year-old boys?

Rose I don't mean now. Anyway, I don't think it's so awful—I mean I've got lots of gay friends, and probably you have as well.

Smale I most certainly have not.

Rose Oh, you have, I bet you have, nice people, I mean, people you like, but you'll never know who because of the way you talk about it.

Malpass I'd much rather not talk about it at all.

Rose Well, better if you never do, because think of the harm you might cause when you do.

Malpass Harm?

Rose How do you know I'm not gay?

Malpass's eyes jerk wide open. Smale is transfixed

Malpass (*hysterically*) Because you're *married*! (*She is really upset*)

Rose stares at her

Rose Sorry.

Rose picks up her "Guardian". Smale soothes Malpass and the Lights dim slightly as Malpass begins to relax to the massage again. The Light comes up on Rose

Rose (*quiet and straight: more to herself than to the audience*) They are my sisters. They are—part of the sisterhood of women. And that's another scene I've buggered up. Mrs Smale and Mrs Malpass. I could actually get quite fond of you if only we talked the same language. I don't seem to be able to manage to talk yours. D'you think you'll ever learn mine?

Pause

Smale She has enthusiasm, I will say that.
Malpass She talks about things that are quite unnecessary.
Smale Her approach to the dinner register can only be described as casual.
Malpass I've been here two years longer than her, who does she think she is applying for deputy headships?
Rose I've got ideas! I want to use them!
Malpass She told me she thinks the reading scheme is boring and sexist!
Rose The only decent character's the dog!
Smale Relationships with colleagues, while friendly, have been marked by a certain lack of tact and reticence.

Pause

Rose Thing is: when Smale comes to write the reference will she yield to temptation and say what she really thinks of me? Or will she write me a really good one to get me off her back?
Smale At present, Mrs Fidgett has neither the dignity nor the experience for a deputy headship.

Smale and Malpass go

Rose rises and comes down

Rose Yeah. *Still.* There is one bright thing. I think my talent may have been spotted from above. From the Office. Yes. "Rose Fidgett, nee Strong, and the Primary Adviser."

The Lights come up

Beam enters and stands watching

Now what have you got on your tables? Work cards, right. Are they ordinary work cards, Rachel? What's the matter with them then? No work on them, right. What? No *work* on the *work* cards? Help? What are we going to do? Yes, we could draw on them. Fine, anything else? We could write on them. Fine, anything else? Yes, we could make paper aeroplanes out of them. Fine. Anything else? You see, what I was thinking was, why is it always *me* doing the work cards and *you* doing the work? Yes, all right, Patrick, because I'm the teacher and you're the children. But what I thought was, you might like to have a go at being the teacher and do some work cards. D'you get it? Think of someone you'd like to do some work for you, and do them a work card. It could be anything you like, draw a rabbit, hard sums, fill in the missing word, write these letters . . . or maybe you could think of a new kind of work card, something I could never think of. You could do one for me if you like. Yes, if you like. (*Looking at Beam*) See if you can think of a question that you know the answer to and I don't. If you rack your brains you'll soon think of one. No, don't tell me. Do me a work card. O.K.? Smashing.

Jim Beam threads his way through the class towards her. He is scruffy—trendy—with big glasses

Beam I hope you didn't mind me sitting in on your lesson, Mrs Strong.
Rose Ms.
Beam Sorry?
Rose Ms Strong.
Beam (*holding out his hand*) Jim Beam.
Rose Rose Strong. Hello.

He takes her hand

Beam I'm the new Primary Adviser.

She lets his hand go

Rose Ah, well, I couldn't really keep you out then, could I?
Beam I'm sorry, I really would have preferred to ask your permission first.
Rose Well, why didn't . . . No, it's all right. Sorry. You feel a bit of a fool. If I'd known you were coming I'd have done something different.
Beam Why?
Rose Oh, all this do your own thing. I gather it's out at the Office.
Beam Ah, now, it is and it isn't. The Office is a great office, and it has many mansions.
Rose Oh.
Beam I like the way you work very much.

There is something quite sexy about all this

Rose Oh. (*Incredulously*) Do you?
Beam I've had a depressing week, in confidence. School after school. "This is a back to the basics school, Mr Beam." "We're not ashamed to say we chant tables here." I've seen so much barking at print this week I could curl up.
Rose I make them chant tables, you know.
Beam Do you?
Rose And put their hands on their heads.
Beam I don't believe you.
Rose Oh, I do. We all do. It's the power, you see. It goes to our heads.
Beam I'll tell you what else you do.
Rose What's that then?

Beam You ask open questions. You're the only teacher I've seen this week who's encouraged pupil-initiated enquiry. You encourage them to predict—to hypothesize.

Rose Oh.

Beam I can tell you've adopted a strategy of planned intervention in their language development.

Rose Can you?

Beam At a glance. You've really absorbed the insights of the Bullock Report, haven't you?

Rose No, I haven't really.

Beam Barnes, Britton and Rosen?

Rose No. *Heard* of them. Not really a language person, I'm a biologist.

Beam I think you're a natural innovator.

Rose Oh. (*To the "class"*) Hey. Dinosaurs! Thought you were being teachers now. Well, do teachers fight over pencils? (*To Beam*) Sorry.

Beam No, no. I'm taking up your time.

Rose It's all right. Don't talk to many grown-ups.

Beam All right if I wander round and have a look at what they're doing?

Rose Feel free.

Beam Thanks. Tell me. Why d'you call them dinosaurs and hamsters and so on?

Rose Oh. Stupid really. The tables choose their own names, whatever they want to be. It's just I got so fed up with red table and blue table and all that.

Beam (*warmly*) Fantastic. (*He moves away*)

Rose Watch out for the dinosaurs. They're a bit primitive.

Beam moves around the tables, looking at work, as it were. Rose draws a deep breath

Hmm (*She feels really pleased, when she thinks about it. Then she knots her brow. To the audience*) Hang on. What *was* all that about? I had the feeling it was some sort of code. Three guesses . . . Not *that* again . . . Five more minutes, folks.

Beam (*to someone sitting at a table*) No, I'm not her dad, I'm another teacher, just come to see all the good work you do. (*As he works his way back to Rose*) I'll come back and see you another day. (*To Rose*) Well, fine. Thanks for having me.

Rose That's O.K.

Beam Look—I'm trying to get together a little working party of like-minded people—share ideas, maybe generate some new ones. I think you might be interested.

Rose Well. I don't know.

Beam I thought we might have a little initial meeting over a drink. Just an informal chat sort of thing. I'd like it if you could come along.

Rose Over a drink sounds promising.

Beam Tuesday?

Rose No, not Tuesday. Sorry.

Beam Ah, fine. Wednesday?

Rose Fine. But look—no, never mind. Where, down the Teachers Centre?
Beam No, I don't think so, do you? D'you know Slops Wine Bar?
Rose Intimately.
Beam Half seven?
Rose Fine.
Beam Smashing. (*About to go*) Well . . .
Rose D'you mind me asking, how many in this group so far?
Beam Not too many. Wednesday?
Rose Fine.
Beam Terrific, see you then.

Beam goes

Rose watches him. During the following, the scene is set for Sally's flat

Rose Excuse me, Ms Strong. What was all that, no, not *Tuesday*? I mean,
I don't always have to go round to my mother's on Tuesdays, no I
just had to say, no, not Tuesday, you don't get old Rose as easy as that
Jim Beam, you've got to put yourself out for something special, but not
all that much, 'cos you can have her Wednesday, I mean, why didn't I
just say, "Tuesday, right, fine! Thank you! Fancy you too!" Or, "Get
lost Beam, get back to the Office and play with your paper clips." (*In
self-parody*) But no, not Tuesday, sorry. Wednesday? Oh, what a girly
game! And after all that probably all he wants is a bloody good rabbit
on about records of reading and "Breakthrough to Literacy", and here
I am getting myself into some . . . *Well*. When things seem to be piling
up on me a bit too fast, I hop in the car and go and see my old mate
Sally. She lives about half an hour away down the bypass. And there she
is and her enormous sofa. And I do mean enormous. Been doing that
ever since we were at college together; somehow we managed to get each
other through all the bad bits and the boring bits, and even, finally, the
finals. And then neither of us taught, not then, but right through the late
sixties, when Sally was singing her songs with Jake Hardman at the
Electric Garden and I was having kids, even then—whenever we met—
it was still O.K.

*Sally, in jeans and a grubby top, and with wild hair, enters and sits on the
sofa*

(*Flopping*) Oh God.
Sally Right.
Rose What's happening?
Sally *Nothing.*
Rose Perfect.
Sally Right.
Rose Oh, I should live in the country.
Sally Yes, it's a riot of colour especially now the flashing season's started.
Rose Eh?
Sally Didn't you know? There's a season for it here. Just about when the
kids start putting their marbles away, that's the flashing season. Around

March the fourteenth it starts. Took me a couple of years to work it out, but it's true.

Rose Go on then.

Sally Well, wet or fine, morning, afternoon and night, the highways and byways and hedges and ditches of Warwickshire start blossoming with honest country yokels dropping their kecks and flashing their compendiums. Don't laugh, I'm serious.

Rose No-one says kecks except you. Or compendiums.

Sally Ar, lass. We'm all got kecks.

Rose But we'm not all got compendiums.

Sally Ar. Nature's a funny old thing.

Rose Ar.

Sally Saw one today, on me way home from the library. Just been giving me chat to the Friends of the Cotswold Countryside about the natural ecology of the English hedgerow.

Rose Oh, I say!

Sally Oh yes, it had gone down a treat, and I was just strolling along, singing a merry song, as is my wont. And then this figure emerged from behind a tree, and adopted a significant pose.

Rose What did you do?

Sally Ah. Well. I'm afraid I played my part badly in this encounter. Thing is, as you know, I can hardly see a thing without my specs, and I didn't have them on. So we both sort of stood there . . . He didn't say anything and I didn't say anything. It seemed to be his move. Funny, I thought. Then I vaguely discerned there was something wrong with his kecks. Has he torn them on some barbed wire, I mused innocently. Is he in need of help? Do I look the sort of lady who carries a needle and thread about with her? So I screwed up me eyes and me courage, and peered closer. And there it was.

Rose His compendium!

Sally Shimmering vaguely through the mist. Blimey, Sally, I thought. Had again!

Rose Oh, Sally. How awful.

Sally Right. One of those really tricky problems in etiquette. I had me specs in me pockets, see. Should I put them on or not? If I did, would he be pleased at my friendly show of interest, or would he be goaded into savage animal lust and it's a long time since I've come across a bit of animal lust—or worst of all, would he think I was trying to make some sort of satirical point about the minuscule dimensions of his compendium?

Rose I'd have thumped him.

Sally You're so decisive, you. In the event, we both sort of stayed where we were, a sort of bucolic tableau, until finally he whisked back behind his tree and did a bit of grunting, and I went on me merry way.

Rose Why do they do it, Sally? Why don't we do it?

Sally A challenging question. Because they're wankers and we're not. And it's not all done behind trees, Rose. Look, the hunt came down that lane last Saturday.

Rose Oh no.

Sally Smashed out of their skulls, skidding down the road like the Charge of the Light Brigade.

Rose Disgusting!

Sally I actually saw the poor old fox nip down the lane, so I shut the gate and sort of leaned on it, and up comes this guy with a purple face on this gigantic charger. "Open this gate, please—quickly." "No." "Open this damn gate!" "Open it yourself, wanker!"

Rose Hurray! (*Or some such approving sound*)

Sally Right. And then he said, "Don't you talk to me like that, get out of my bloody way!" Just like that. But I kept my dignity: "Piss off, wanker" I said. "Go and chase something you own size!"

Rose Great!

Sally (*more hesitantly*) And then—he just sort of stared at me. He had this look of—*mad hatred* in his eyes—and he got off his horse and walked right up to me with his whip. He really wanted to hit me with it. I thought I was going to piss myself, Rose. I had to get out of his way. They really hate us, you know. I think they really do hate us.

Rose Not all of them, Sally.

Sally No?

Rose Half the human race, you know.

Sally (*cheerfully*) Right.

Rose Ah well, look, it's all right for you to think that. Living here.

Sally Right.

Rose I mean I . . .

Sally You can be honest with me, Rose. Only old Sally.

Rose I was just thinking . . . I dunno. Like this morning, I was late going out to school again, and old Geoff was blocking up the bathroom, I only wanted to squeeze by him and get a quick swill. He wouldn't move. I was just sort of standing there looking at his back. His hard old back. He didn't like me in there with him. I was almost scared to squeeze by him, it was really nasty.

Sally Right.

Rose Then he turned round. D'you know what he'd been doing?

Sally What?

Rose Straightening the toothpaste tube. And there was me . . . (*She lets out a laugh and stops when she sees Jake*)

Jake totters in like a man in a dream. He stops and stares at Rose

Hello, Jake.

Jakes stares at Rose for a long time

Jake Susan

Sally Oh, Jake!

Jake No. (*He holds up his hand to stop her telling him*) Rose.

Rose That's it. How are you, Jake?

Jake (*not sure*) All right. All right.

Rose Seems to me you might be a little bit stoned.

Sally Blimey, hear that infant teacher coming out. You've got to watch that.

Jake What?

Sally She's an infant teacher.

Jake To teach infants—must be the purest delight. But what do you teach them?

Rose Oh, you know. Read and write.

Jake I wish I had never learnt to read or write.

Sally Jake, are you looking for something?

Jake A Bible—I was looking for a Bible.

Sally Come here, sit down, now. You burnt it. Don't you remember? You took it to read on that picnic and then you lit the fire with it.

He stares at her, trying to remember

Jake It doesn't matter.

He sits down between them and goes to sleep almost instantly. Sally puts an absent-minded affectionate hand on him

Sally Sorry.

He shifts and gets more comfortable

Rose Is he all right?

Sally Ah, yeah, he's got this gift of taking a catnap whenever he needs one. Mark of a great man that, Winston Churchill was just the same, Napoleon, all them.

Rose Oh, Sally.

Sally Actually, it's not the stuff so much these days, he's got this craze on Southern Comfort. Bloody expensive, but he can afford it. Wish he couldn't. Just these six songs, he could live the rest of his life on the royalties. However long that is, et cetera.

Sally is a different person with and about Jake: tender, protective, easily hurt. Rose goes carefully

Rose How—*is* the music?

Sally Oh, fine. Not bad. We're working a bit. We're doing Alcester Folk Club Saturday.

Rose Alcester *Folk Club*?

Sally Yeah.

Rose (*taking a quick look at Jake to make sure he is asleep*) But you used to do . . . Well, Jake used to do . . .

Sally Yeah. We're unreliable now. The word is well round. It's only stage-fright, Rose. But it's spread. First it was just really big concerts he couldn't do unless he was stoned, then any stage appearance, then he had this big block about asking for things in shops.

Jake wakes up suddenly, apparently sober and alert

Jake What's the time?

Sally About half-five.

Jake Shit, is it? I've got to practise. Nice seeing you, Rose. Stay for a meal. We can talk.

Rose I'm not sure if I can, Jake.

Jake You stay. You know I like to talk to you. Stay for a meal. Now I have to practise.

Jake goes

Sally Now he has to practise drinking. He hasn't got through a meal this week. Fine old performance, head in the plate by half-past nine. Don't stay. It's—tedious for guests.

Rose Sally!

Sally Used to yearn for him at concerts all those years. Used to think, if only I could be with Jake Hardman, I could understand. If only I could get the kecks off him. And then I did, and honest, it was like I thought— he was the most—the *only* really sensitive man I've ever met. He's so sensitive now he can't go and buy a packet of fags on his own. We still make love, well I make it to him. He's no tiger. But we do manage.

Rose Sounds all right.

Sally You should see us. I feel bad talking like this. I still love him. And he wrote six standards. *Six.* But I'm going to have to kick him out. I know that, Rose.

Pause

Rose New man came into my life today.

Sally (*snapping out of it*) Ah! Now you're talking? Did you pull him?

Rose Not there and then in the classroom. That's where it was.

Sally But you're going to pull him.

Rose I don't know. He was very tentative.

Sally Well, they all are these days, you don't want to stand for that. What was he like? Did he have a big dick?

Rose Amazing.

Sally You stand no nonsense from him then. Get his kecks off.

Rose He had a nice face too.

Sally Now don't you start turning into a face woman, Rosie Fidgett, you can't afford to weaken. Start getting soft with them, they take advantage, use their little wheedling ways with you, and before you know where you are, you're caught. Like me.

Rose And me. I have got this husband, you know.

Sally Oh, yes. Keep forgetting him.

Rose So do I. The little man.

Sally The old ball and chain.

Rose Nice to have someone to come home to though.

Sally So long as you keep 'em right there.

Rose And they love you for it.

Sally Toss 'em the odd word.

Rose }
Sally } (*together*) { Shut up!

Rose Bit of a cuddle now and then.

Sally But you can't let 'em trap you.
Rose You got to be hard with them.
Sally Cruel to be kind.
Rose Only language they understand.
Sally As for this guy, you've got to put it straight. Look, you've got a sweet face, but I'm a married woman.
Rose I've got a family and responsibilities.
Sally We could be great together, but no emotional involvement.
Rose Not the starry-eyed type.
Sally I'll be frank, you know my motto about men?

Rose
Sally } *(together)* { Find 'em, feel 'em, fuck 'em, and forget 'em!

Pause. They subside

Sally Seriously, though, do it, Rose.
Rose D'you reckon? D'you think that's the answer?
Sally Oo, ar. Wouldn't go as far as that. But look at it this way: what else is there to do? While you've still got most of your own teeth like.
Rose Ar.
Sally Ar.
Rose Ar.

Rose comes away

Sally goes

During the following, the scene is set for Rose and Geoffrey's house, and then Geoffrey comes in

Rose Sally does exhilarate me. "I'm going to have to kick him out." What an exhilarating phrase. I love stuff like that. There was this poem they made us read once, how did it go: "He walked out on the whole crowd" leaves me flushed and stirred. Like "then she undid her dress" or, "take that, you bastard!" But "I'm going to have to kick him out", that's the best of the lot. I like the drive home, too: country lanes first, then bombing along the bypass, carving it up with all those little reps in their Escorts. I think it's a smashing road, that bypass, I won't have a word said against it. And I'm thinking I'm going to have to kick him out, hell, Sally can do it, I can do it, and my foot's hard down on the floor and the road ahead is clear, vroom! And then I'm slowing up for the roundabout, and it's all changing down and thirty mile limit, and what a careful lady I've become. There's a sign just before you get to our estate that's always puzzled me; it says, dead slow, altered priorities ahead. And dead slow my little car obediently goes, nosing down our avenue, past the weeping cherries, into the car-port, snug as a hamster, and I switch off and the engine dies. What are you like with your husband? This is what we're like.

Geoffrey is sitting at the table, working

Rose comes in

Rose Sorry, sorry I'm late.
Geoffrey Fine. No problem.
Rose I went to see Sally. I left a note for the kids.
Geoffrey I read it.
Rose I tried to phone you . . .
Geoffrey Did you?
Rose No. I nearly did but then I just went. Sorry. Are you cross?
Geoffrey No.
Rose I mean, if you are, do say. I would.
Geoffrey Nothing to be cross about. Everything's fine. I coped.
Rose Kids all right?
Geoffrey Fine.
Rose You're a good lad.
Geoffrey Thank you.
Rose Where are they?
Geoffrey Sarah's watching telly.
Rose Done her flute practice?
Geoffrey (*wearily*) Yes.
Rose What about Alex?
Geoffrey Homework. He's only just gone up. He had whatsisname, Huggie, round earlier. Swapping things, or selling things. Don't worry. Everything's fine.
Rose Sure?

She means "sure you feel all right about it?" He takes it as meaning "sure you could manage?"

Geoffrey (*implying a tinge of irritated contempt*) There's not a lot to tax the brain about getting supper and washing it up, Rose. About two minutes thought and ten minutes effort I'd say.
Rose Well, that's super.
Geoffrey I mean, if I couldn't apply critical path analysis I'd soon be up shit creek at work, wouldn't I? There's a problem, and a time to solve it in. The problem's hunger, right?

We sense how boring and narrow he can be at work

The special circumstances are that the time factor's crucial. Because there's been a breakdown at stage one. Buying the raw material. Right?
Rose We had eggs.
Geoffrey We didn't feel like eating eggs.
Rose Intrusion of consumer resistance?
Geoffrey If you like, Rose. So we needed to come up with something that had a very short A to B factor, but would still satisfy the basic specification.
Rose So what did you come up with?
Geoffrey Sent Alex down the chip shop.
Rose Ah! Brilliant.
Geoffrey I mean, it bloody amuses me the mystique some women make out of what's basically such a mundane area. All that house stuff, it's so

trivial, Rose, all it wants is a bit of applied analysis and you can see it
off in no time, give yourself room for something a bit more important.
Rose Yes, I see, thank you, Geoffrey.
Geoffrey No trouble.
Rose What's more important tonight then?
Geoffrey Well, I do happen to have a hell of a lot of paperwork to shift
tonight.
Rose Oh. Sorry.
Geoffrey Just sorting one of Targett's little schemes for him.
Rose Oh. I was hoping we might have a bit of a chat.
Geoffrey Yes, well, fine. I'll see what I can do. About how long were you
thinking?

She looks at him

Rose Hadn't actually worked it out in minutes.
Geoffrey I have got quite a bit to shift.
Rose Tough day at work, was it?
Geoffrey Nothing that can't be sorted.

Pause. She starts to speak but he is into his stride

See, first thing this morning, Targett lands a file this thick on my desk.
"Be grateful if you could skim through that Geoffrey, welcome any of
your insights that float to the surface", you know how these prats talk.
And then half an hour later, little Anderson's in to take it away again,
get a few flimsies run off. "Have it with my blessings," I said.
Rose Geoff. Look. Um—when I was coming back from Sally's . . .
Geoffrey No, I haven't come to it yet. Half way through the afternoon,
Targett's back. "Had time to browse and ruminate, Geoffrey?" "Don't
see how I could," I said, "you had it back off me half an hour after you
put it down there." "Surely not." "Ask Anderson," I said. "He took it
off to the copy room." "Oh. Really? I'm so sorry, you're absolutely right."
"I know I'm right," I said. "Well, I shall have to start writing myself
memos . . . if I can remember what to say, eh?" Prat. That's the guy
they bring in over me, that's the systems expert. His bloody secretary's
got an honours degree. "Oh well, Geoffrey, it doesn't matter really. It'll
be exciting to have your first impressions at the meeting tomorrow." I
should smile. I'm going to crack it tonight from first principles.
Rose So you've got a lot of work on.
Geoffrey I've just been—no, never mind. I can cope.
Rose I was listening, honest. (*Pause*) Actually if you're working I can
have a crack at that reading scheme.
Geoffrey Oh yes? Good dog, Nip, eh?
Rose Come, Nip, come! See! Nip comes. He's about the only one who
bloody does. It's a terrible world in these reading schemes, Geoff.
Geoffrey Oh, yeah. (*He has heard it before*)
Rose Peter will help Daddy wash the car. See Jane dust with Mummy.
Geoffrey Bit dull, yeah.
Rose Bit dull, it's bloody criminal. Wait till I get mine out! Jane likes to

fight. Peter has a new doll. Mum is out. Mum likes fun. She is fond of a
treat. Dad will get the chips. Dad can crack it. Dad can cope fine.

Little pause

Geoffrey Are you in for the night then, now?
Rose Yes, I think so.
Geoffrey I was thinking I might go out for a drink when I've shifted that
lot.
Rose Do. You owe it to yourself. Unless you fancy staying home.
Geoffrey What?
Rose I thought we might have an evening in. Drink a bottle of wine.
Couple of bottles.
Geoffrey It's a bad night on the box.
Rose I meant . . . (*She is embarrassed*) I mean we could—sort of have an
evening together. You know. *Talk* and that.
Geoffrey Oh. (*Trying to muster a response to this surprising suggestion*)
Yes! Fine! If you like . . .
Rose It's all right, you don't have to.
Geoffrey (*seizing*) Your mother was round earlier. She thought you'd be
in. Of course I wasn't able to tell her where you were.
Rose What did she want?
Geoffrey I don't know.
Rose What did she say?
Geoffrey She said I hope she remembers she's married.
Rose Oh. S'pose I'd better go round and see her. If I go now, you could
go out for a drink a bit later.
Geoffrey Right. Unless you really want an evening in.
Rose No. It's all right. It really doesn't matter.
Geoffrey Fine.

*Rose stands looking at Geoffrey. He looks up and she looks back at him
before he turns away*

The Lights concentrate on Rose

   Geoffrey exits

Rose (*reflectively*) I'm really going to have to kick you out, Geoffrey.

*Pause. During the following, the scene is set for the Classroom and
then Malpass comes in*

I love week-ends, don't you? Zero structure, re-discovery time, and all
that crap in the Sunday papers. What a lot of paperwork we shifted on
Friday night, not to mention pints, and I chalked up a good ninety
minutes credit round at mum's on the unnecessary ways of the woman
next door and what she thinks *her* aim is, and Saturday I really gave
Sainsbury's a fearful hammering and Geoffrey watched not one but two
rugby internationals on television, while boys in ten-hole Docs and
Harringtons hurtled in and out of the house stamping and growling at
each other and girls with flutes wafted up and down the stairs, and

somehow in the middle of all that, even while indulging in the odd furtive thought about Primary Advice, I could still feel the old surge of warm family life flood over me, and there I was again on Saturday night thinking it could still somehow be fine, and there was nothing wrong with us that a couple of Hungarian Rieslings and a bit of collusive fantasy couldn't put right, but even as I snuggled up to Geoffrey while he watched four hysterical middle-aged gentlemen arguing about Kevin Keegan, I felt his back go hard as an old crab clinging to a rock . . . and I limped upstairs defeated to my pit . . . And *Sunday* round to lunch my *mother* came like *always*, and like always she made absolutely no bones at all about what a *disgrace* the weather had been *all week*, and I was so *nice* and *calm* and *patient* I could feel some sort of big soft explosion welling up inside my head and I dragged poor old Sarah off for a long trudge in a muddy wood that she could well have done without. As we came back, I looked through the window, and saw my husband, becalmed at his desk. And I had this sudden disturbing memory of something I'd seen in a film about Darwin—a giant turtle fossil welded to a rock in the Galapagos Islands. (*Pause. Then she speaks pointedly to the audience*) The thing about school is that you have to go there every day. It's the only way they have of doing it. And that's quite nice, knowing where you have to be, that that's where they are, the kids, and the teachers all in it together.

The Lights come up on Malpass who is sitting in an armchair in the Staffroom putting on lipstick. She has a file of papers with her

Rose comes in and Malpass puts the lipstick away as if she is ashamed of it

Rose Oh, God, Monday.
Malpass I'm sorry?
Rose Nothing. Just, Monday. You know.
Malpass Oh. (*Making an effort*) Yes, I know.
Rose Though, that's an awful thing to say, I mean, there they are, they really look forward to seeing us, some of them, we should . . .
Malpass Yes.
Rose How's the headache now? I mean, the migraine.
Malpass (*tight*) Much better, thank you.
Rose Really?
Malpass Yes, really; much better.
Rose I'm—sorry if I upset you, Friday. I've been thinking about it.
Malpass (*unconvincingly*) You didn't upset me.
Rose No, it was rotten. I didn't mean to. I mean, it's enough of a strain, being with the kids all day—I don't know what your husband does, but mine goes and sits in an office, and a girl brings him coffee, and if he wants to, he can go out for half an hour, and nobody comes and plagues him for spellings, nobody's sick on the floor, not even at the office party . . .
Malpass Rolls-Royce.

Rose What?

Malpass My husband works there.

Rose Oh, yes. In the office?

Malpass Drawing Office.

Rose Yes, well, there you are. They don't know.

Malpass They don't know *anything*. (*She has come out too much and feels the need to withdraw: she finds some physical way of doing it*)

Rose So, really, I mean, I'm sorry. It's a hard life, we ought to stick together.

Malpass You don't seem to find it hard. You just—sail through it.

Rose I don't. Honest. I'm whistling in the dark. I think I know what's right to do but people keep telling me I'm wrong, and bloody parents come up and say I'm very worried about Sharon, and I think that's *her child*, and what have I done about Sharon except hear her read and stop Garth hitting her, and so on, multiplied by *thirty-five*.

Malpass I didn't know you felt like that.

Rose Well I do. But then I think we all do but we feel we've got to hide it—it's as if there's something stopping you from being yourself when you're in school, and that's not right—is it? I mean, it should be possible to let things show—even weaknesses, I think the kids could take it.

Malpass I don't think I could do that. (*Fiddling nervously with a paper from her file*) Not sure that I could.

Rose Hey, that's good! (*Indicating the paper—a drawing*) Can I have a look?

Malpass is not displeased

That's smashing.

Malpass D'you think so?

Rose Is that your dog?

Malpass Yes. (*Pause*) Sheba.

Rose I didn't even know you had a dog. Did you do it?

Malpass No, Derek did. My husband. He's always drawing her.

Rose Really? It's so delicate, you know.

Malpass I thought I'd show it to the children.

Rose Yeah. And then you could bring her in person, next week!

Malpass Oh, I couldn't do that.

Rose They'd love it. You could always make 'em do some creative writing about her, pass it off as work, like. You could tell Mrs Smale it's recommended in the Bullock Report. Dare say it is.

Malpass I wouldn't know. (*Like most infant teachers, Malpass feels threatened by the Bullock Report*)

Rose Nor would I, to be honest. Hey, look, did you meet the Primary Adviser bloke on Friday?

Malpass He did come in.

Rose He was nice, wasn't he? Well, he seemed all right to me. He stayed and talked for quite a bit, he seemed really sympathetic. He's trying to get some sort of discussion group going, starting Wednesday. Why don't you come?

Malpass Oh no, I don't think I could. It's Derek's snooker night and I usually do my hair and have an early night.

Rose Well, let him do his hair for once on a Wednesday. Come on, why not? I'm going.

Malpass I'm not applying for deputy headships.

Rose It's not that. It's a chance to talk, get ideas, get things, you know, off your chest . . .

Malpass It's not my sort of thing.

Rose You could make it your sort of thing. And he's not like the rest of that lot, he's a human being, he's nice.

Malpass (*very tight*) If it's of any interest to you, he stood at the back of my classroom for ten minutes and walked out without saying a word!

Malpass exits and the Lights concentrate on Rose

Rose In my line of business you often come across stories about little girl animals, who set off to see the world, have adventures, take control, put themselves about a bit, you know. And they always, always find that the world is full of scary foxes and big, bad wolves, and they are jolly glad to scamper back to the cosy farm. It is not like that, it is not like that! All the foxes are frightened and all the wolves round here are on valium. I open the gate and I say "Hello world, Rose here" and all you can see for miles are furry bums disappearing down burrows. I do not mean any harm, I just want things to be real. Where is everybody? I just want to be myself, that's all. Will someone tell me what's so frightening about that? (*Pause. Quietly*) I just felt like talking to someone, that's all.

The Lights come up off stage as Mother, Malpass, Beam, Jake, Smale and Geoffrey speak from the doorways as at the opening of the Act

Mother I know it's not for me, it's just to make you feel better!

Malpass (*quietly and deadly*) You can't help me. I'm not like you.

Beam You've really absorbed the insights of the Bullock Report haven't you?

Jake I wish I'd never learnt to read and write.

Smale Work to do, work to do.

Geoffrey Critical path—not to worry, it's all cracked—forget it.

Sally I'm really going to have to kick him out.

Malpass And we're supposed to educate children in an atmosphere like that.

Rose Look, this is not fair.

Geoffrey (*wearily*) No problem. I sent Alex down the chip shop.

Rose And what do *you* want?

Geoffrey It's all right. It really doesn't matter.

Rose (*after a long pause*) Fine.

The Lights fade to Black-out and—

the CURTAIN *falls*

ACT II

The Lights come up on Rose and Geoffrey's bedroom

Rose is sitting at her dressing-table, making up. Her mother sits on the bed, in hat and coat, watching her

Mother I'll tell you what, Rose, you want to get that bit of wood fixed downstairs by your front door.

Rose Do I?

Mother Yes, you want to get that fixed soon. It's all loose, I keep thinking I'm going to fall over it, and it makes the door stick. And it's going to bring the edge of the carpet up soon if it's not done. I notice it's fraying now.

Rose *(moaning)* Oohhhhh.

Mother Well, it won't do itself, will it?

Rose I was hoping it might sort of settle down of its own accord.

Mother It's going to ruin that carpet *and* force the hinges loose on your front door, *and* someone's going to trip over it and have a nasty fall. Mrs Garbey's next door was like that, and I told her you want to get that seen to, and she said I'm meaning to, and then she fell over it herself and broke her shoulder. I went to see her in hospital and she said you were quite right, I should have listened to you. I took her one of those cakes from Elizabeth the Chef but I don't think she ate it. I hate waste. All you want is a couple of screws!

Rose Oh, Mother, is that really all I want?

Mother No need to be sarky with me, you don't suit it, never did.

Rose Sorry.

Mother I date it from the time you stopped calling me mummy and started this mother business.

Rose You called your mother "Mother".

Mother Well, we did then. Has Geoffrey got a countersink punch?

Rose Has Geoffrey got a what?

Mother A countersink punch.

Rose Gosh, I don't know. I rather doubt it.

Mother Because unless he countersinks those screws they'll stick up and catch the door and he'll have achieved *nothing*! Your father always used to countersink his screws. You want to tell Geoffrey to be sure and countersink his screws, or they'll catch the door.

Rose I knew there was something I wanted to tell him but I didn't realize it was that!

Mother You know I don't mean to interfere, Rose.

Rose Sorry.

Mother I was just trying to give you a hint.

Rose Yes, I know, I ought to have a go at it. Stuff like that, I just wish it would go away, and little jobs seem to depress old Geoff out of all proportion.

Mother He does want to get that job done though.

Rose No, Mother, he doesn't. If the door jammed shut for ever he'd just walk round the back. Why don't *you* ask him?

Mother (*shocked*) Oh, I couldn't do that. (*Pause, then as if discussing an embarrassing disability*) He's not very mechanically minded, is he?

Rose No.

Mother No. Still, I suppose some men aren't. (*Pause*) We were forty years in that house in Melton Avenue and we never had to have a man in.

Rose I know.

Mother Ours was the only house that had its guttering cleaned out twice a year. The only one.

Rose Mm.

Mother And then it didn't seem to add anything to the value when we came to sell it. Will he be wanting to come in?

Rose Who?

Mother Your husband.

Rose Well, if he does, I expect he will.

Mother I mean, will he want to get changed.

Rose Well, if he does, he will.

Mother I don't want to be in the way.

Rose You're not in the way.

Mother I can't seem to get relaxed tonight. (*Picking up a dress from the bed*) Is this what you're wearing?

Rose Mm. Thought so.

Mother Is it a dance then?

Rose I told you, it's a *meeting*.

Mother Not much of that for a meeting, is there. You'll catch your death, that's thinner than what we'd wear to the dances in the Oxford Rooms. Why don't you wear, that other thing, that jersey dress, I'd have thought you'd have suited that better for a meeting. Still I don't know what these meetings are like.

Rose Not sure I do.

Mother Will there be many there?

Rose Not a lot, I gather.

Mother Don't you think you go to too many of these meetings, you hardly ever seem to stop home these days. I don't know what you'd do without me to baby-sit. Baby-sit. Alex is bigger than me!

Rose They love having you here. Honest.

Mother Yes, well, if that's all I'm any use for I might as well do it; still, I'm surprised you want to turn out on a night like this, after working all day, you must be fond of a treat.

Rose I am.

Mother Yes, well, so long as you remember you're married.

Rose pulls a face

I was wearing one a bit like that when I met your father. That was in the Oxford Rooms. He was a lovely dancer. Very light on his feet. Well, he always wore his pumps. Not all of them did, but he did. I was longing for him to ask me to dance, and then he did, it was the Moonlight Saunter, I can remember it now, we hadn't got twice round the room before I felt something give.

Rose What?

As Mother gets into her story it becomes clear what a bright young girl she was

Mother The elastic on my drawers. It happened that quick they were down round my ankles before you could say knife. Step out of them, he said. Quick as that. I can hear him now. Step out of them. And I did, and he had them in his pocket that quick no-one knew what was going on. But I couldn't look him in the face after that, could I? I managed to keep going round just till that dance was finished, like, just so nobody would notice anything, and then I ran away to hide from him, spent the whole evening in the ladies cloakroom. Nobody knew what was the matter with me.

Rose Oh, Mother.

Mother But at the end he was waiting for me on the steps. I've got something of yours, you know, he said. You didn't think I'd let you go without me, did you? And he just took my arm. He never told anybody about it, you know, Rose. He was a real gentleman.

Rose Was it—um . . . (*It is difficult, but she feels she has rarely been this close*) Was it very good with him?

Mother Well, Rose, you know I thought the world of him. Oh, I see, you mean what they call the physical side. Well, I don't think we bothered so much about all that then. He was a very shy man, you know, Rose, very modest. I was myself.

Rose I used to think, you know, he was sort of against all that.

Mother Oh, no. Mind you, like I say, he was a very modest man. I sometimes used to wish he was more . . . But there, you can't wish for the moon. He never badly used me, you know, and he was never . . . I think in a way he set too much store by it, if you know what I mean, Rose.

Rose Yes.

The Lights concentrate on Rose, and her father's voice is heard, off, at a time when she was sixteen

Father (*off*) Rose, is that you? (*Basically, he is scared*) How was I to know you were in? Creeping up the stairs. You know your mother can't sleep when you're out late. Not till one o'clock in the morning, not at your age. And I'd have got the strap if I had. You know very well why. You dirty little bugger.

There is the sound of a slap and it is evident that he has hit her across the face. It hurts. Rose puts her hand to her face and the Lights come up full again

Mother He was very fond of you, your dad. Nothing was too good for our little Rose.

Rose I know.

Mother I keep thinking Geoffrey'll be wanting to come in.

Rose Well, if he does he will.

Mother I mean he'll want to get changed. He might want to change his trousers, Rose.

Rose We might get lucky.

Mother Well, it wouldn't do for me to see him in his birthday suit, now would it?

Rose I don't suppose he'd mind, Mother.

Mother No, they don't now, do they? You know, your father would never let me see him naked. He was very modest about that, he'd always lock the bathroom door, except, you know, the last couple of years. It seems a shame in a way, Rose, he had a lovely build.

Rose Yes, I know.

Mother Not till right near the end, you know, when I had to wash him and change him and everything. I think that was the first time I'd ever got a proper look at him, and even then, you know, when I had to wash his, you know, his peenuss, even when he was helpless, he'd try to brush my hand off, he thought it was all wrong—(*unconsciously doing the brushing off movement*)—and I almost had to laugh, of course it hadn't been any danger for years. We'd been brought up to think it was ugly, Rose, but it wasn't ugly, really, not even then. They're quite bonny really when you get your eye in for them, don't you think, Rose? Seemed such a waste. Are you laughing at me?

Rose No, I'm not. You never said anything like that to me before.

Mother Yes, well, doesn't matter what I say now, does it like?

Rose Wish you had before.

Mother Yes, well, we didn't then, did we? Mind, I think it's best now what you young ones do, talk it out in the open. And I'm fond of a bit crack. Well, it puts the time in. I'm stopping you getting on, and your husband'll want to get changed. I'll go down to see to the bairns now, Rose.

Rose Mum, d'you ever think—well, that it's all been set up so that no-one gets what they want?

Mother Well, of course it is, the secret's not expecting too much from it. Eh, is that the time, I've missed *Crossroads*.

Mother goes

Rose sighs

Rose Oh, Mother. Talking was never your problem. You always seemed to be able to decide what you'd say and when. It's me. I can talk a bit to the kids, I can talk a bit to Sally, but I can't say things to Geoffrey, it's too hard when you've been married so long. And I could never in a million years say—(*with great force and conviction*)—"Oh, Mother, can't you see, you may have a dead husband, but I've got a dead marriage!" (*Pause*) Silly bugger. Dead marriage. Sounds like a dead hamster. Darling. Yes, darling? Can you smell something funny under the sideboard, darling? Oh, don't worry, darling, it's only a dead marriage. Anyway, our marriage is not dead. It's only half-dead.

Geoffrey comes in, He has been having a bath and is wearing a short, old, cheap-looking shiny dressing-gown over nothing. He comes and stands behind her, stooping to comb his hair in the imaginary mirror

Oh, I say, you do look spruce.

Geoffrey Ha.

Rose You must be the cleanest man in the Midlands tonight. You were in there so long I thought you were going to soak your toenails off.

Geoffrey (*in a hollow voice*) Ha, ha ha ha ha. (*He sits on the bed and sort of goes into a vacant trance*)

Rose cranes to see him in the mirror

Rose Right little barrel of fun tonight. Come on, it can't be that bad. What's on for tonight, then?

Geoffrey (*very quickly*) Meeting.

Rose Oh.

Geoffrey What have you got on tonight?

Rose Meeting.

Geoffrey Ah.

Rose That's that, then. (*To the audience*) I will say this for him, he does look after his clothes. He's had that ratty old dressing-gown ever since I've known him. He proposed to me in that dressing-gown.

During the following, Geoffrey goes and lies down behind the bed so that he is unseen by the audience

That was in what I think of as my mucky period. I was a keen young biology student, and I used to go and visit him in this flat. Ooh, what a mucky flat it was. We'd just lie about, him and me, me and my dirty lover in his dirty room, and I loved it, I was really being the dirty little bugger my dad said I was, and it was nice, I really really loved him and his flat, I think he hoped I'd clean it up for him, but I wasn't having that, I liked it just as it was, him and me, lying about in the dust and gloom being dirty—and then one day he proposed to me.

Rose goes and joins Geoffrey so that they are both lying behind the bed. There are satisfied noises of "Oh yes!" Then Geoffrey feels on the bed for the cigarettes and lighter. He sits up, lights a cigarette, lies down again and hands the cigarette to Rose. He sits up again, looks down and then looks very worried. He begins searching around on the bed

Geoffrey Oh, Christ.

Rose What?

Geoffrey Well, I seem to have lost it.

Rose What?

Geoffrey (*after having a brief look*) Seems to have come off inside you.

Rose (*puzzled*) Eh? (*Realizing*) What? (*Leaping up from behind the bed*) What are we going to do? I've got to wash it out!
Geoffrey I don't think you can do that!
Rose Well, I've got to do something!
Geoffrey Probably be all right.
Rose Oh, Geoffrey! I'm going down the bathroom!
Geoffrey O.K.
Rose Well, come with me then.
Geoffrey You know where it is.
Rose Oh, you mean bugger, you know I'm frightened of that geyser.
Geoffrey It's simple.
Rose Well, come with me then. We've got to be quick.

He does not move

Oh, you mean bugger.

Rose rushes off

Geoffrey lights a cigarette. Pause

(*Off*) Geoffrey, I can't find the matches.
Geoffrey On the window sill.

Pause then Geoffrey jumps off the bed

Rose totters back on

Rose It exploded. You mean bugger. You wouldn't come with me. (*She is shaking*)
Geoffrey It's all right. We'll get married.

They stand still for a moment facing each other, then Geoffrey sits down on the bed again slowly. Rose goes back to the mirror

Rose (*to herself*) Yes. And I could have said no, but as my mother said, with a bairn on the way your choices are a bit cut down like, and my father wouldn't speak to me at all for months and well, I did love him and his dust and his dressing-gown. (*To Geoffrey*) Come on, it can't be that bad. Get your trousers on. (*She holds them out*)

Geoffrey gets up, grabs the trousers and goes out

Rose picks up the dress and pulls it on. During the following, the scene is set for Slops Wine Bar

Trouble with you, Rose, you want it all on a plate, don't you? Yes. That would be a very convenient way of having it. Always ready with a slick answer. Don't you realize you've got to work at your marriage? We have done, we have done. We've always done our own servicing. Handbook, good set of spanners and sockets, you can fix anything. Coming down the pub for a jar, Geoffrey? No, no, Saturday mornings we always do a bit of work on the old marriage, you know. It's a kind of hobby with us. Never happier than when I'm greasing the old nipples, y'know. Oh, yes. Any time you liked, you could come round and see us working on our marriage. You know. Lying underneath it with our feet sticking out. Only in recent years have we had to seek any outside help. Oh, Rose. Who's going to fancy you in that? Jim Beam the Primary School Adviser, that's who. Think positive. (*She squirts perfume, on her neck, behind her ears, down the front of her dress and on an afterthought at the top of her thighs*)

Rose goes out of the room, switching off the light as she goes

Wine bar music is heard

The Lights come up very slowly, Rose is sitting at the table

Beam enters, carrying a bottle, and sits at the table

Rose Another *bottle*?

Beam Well, you know the sort of stuff they sell by the glass.

Rose Oh, yes. Casa Rotaguta. Well, this is very nice. I ought to pay for this one though.

Beam Oh, no no no.

Rose Are we on expenses?

Beam I have a Puritan conscience about expenses.

Rose And everything else, I trust. Funny how the rest of the like-minded people didn't show up.

Beam It seems like-minded people are few and far between in this town.

Rose *People* are few and far between in this town. Grown-up people, anyway. (*She looks around*) D'you know I think we might be the only ones in this place of legal drinking age? Go on, pour away. I've got hollow legs.

Beam The girl at the bar said a strange thing to me—I asked her if she had any nuts! Do you know what she said? "Do I look as if I've got any nuts!" No, it's very disturbing that for the linguistic philosopher.

Rose Sounds to me as if you might be in there, I'll keep your seat if you like!

Beam No thanks! I'm fine where I am. (*Pause as he pours a drink*) Actually, I think my Puritan conscience can square with the *first* bottle on expenses. This one's personal.

Rose Does that mean we can stop talking about language development in the integrated day now?

Beam If we like, yes.

Rose What's all this about, then?

He takes a drink

Beam You're very direct, aren't you?

Rose Weren't they like that in Bristol?

Beam Oh, no. Very devious, Bristolians.

Rose Sorry. I didn't used to be like this. I am now though. With new people. It's my policy. It's only with new people, I can't be like this with the old ones. You get trapped in these games and routines and you can't get out of them.

Beam How's it working out so far?

Rose What?

Beam Being direct, with the new people.

Rose I dunno yet, you're the first. What's it all about then?

Beam Well—it's about pleasure, I suppose. Um—getting to know each other. Feeling our way? (*He drinks more*)

Rose I've accelerated your alcohol consumption. And you haven't even said anything yet.

Beam But it is like that. Isn't that how it has to be?

Rose I dunno, I hoped there might be some other way.

Beam (*taking her hand*) You're very nice, you know. I'm very glad I met you.

She looks at their hands, looks at him, begins to speak, hesitates, strokes his hand with the other hand, changes her mind, speaks after all

Rose Yes, I s'pose you're quite right, really. I mean you can't just fall on me like King Rat even supposing you wanted to. I mean we have to send out these little messages in code and see if we like the feel of each other's hands and see if we laugh at the same jokes, even though it's very hard to listen to what's coming out of our mouths. Because the main thing on our minds is does she do it and will she for me, and will she tonight, sorry if I'm being embarrassing and barking up the wrong tree if that's the right phrase, because I'm just extrapolating from my own feelings, just ordinary woman feelings like do I look all right and does he actually fancy me or is he just pretending or is he just being polite, and if not is he going to make a move and if so when's he going to make it. See?

Beam (*smiling*) Go on.

Rose Well, you see, all that implies that we've got to sit here in this alcoholic youth club and finish up all that wine and maybe even a brandy or two until they turn on those horrible interrogation-type spotlights they have in all these places, and we're caught in the glare like a police raid or something, and then we know it's really time to go, and you really have to say something, or not, or maybe I have to say something, but let's assume it's you, because you seem to be the sort of guy who takes charge, you are the Primary Adviser after all.

Beam So what do I say?

Rose Well, let's see, you are the Primary Adviser and a devious Bristolian so you can't say Rose, I'd really like to shaft you or anything like that, no, it'll still be in code, like have you got time for a coffee back at my place, right? And I won't say what for, I've got plenty of coffee at home and anyway I prefer a cup of tea after I've been drinking, no, I wouldn't do any of that, I'd say mm, yes, that would be very nice, and give you one of those code smiles, and you'd think pow! Beam scores again! Or does he? Because there's still lots and lots to go through, like when we get outside and there's two cars and not one, now do I follow you in my car or do we both go in yours? Tricky, that, because if we take the two cars you won't have to turn out afterwards and take me back to the car park, and that could be a very sticky journey as well as inconvenient if the stuff at your place didn't turn out according to plan, but then again, if we both go in the one car at least we know I'm going to get to the place, and we can hold hands on the way and create some sort of atmosphere of pleasurable expectancy, although we're both furiously thinking our own thoughts all the way, and you keep having to let go of my hand to change gear.

Beam My car is automatic!

Rose Ah, well, I can see you've made your mind up about the transport arrangements then. So there we are back at your place, and the door closes behind us, and then what? Do you take me in your arms straight away, or do you bustle off and actually make this coffee you've been talking about? Well, maybe both, first one, then the other, cos you've got class, you're not a bull at a gate man, I can see that, so off you go to make the coffee and I wander round have a look at your books and that, until I get lonely and nervous after about thirty seconds and follow you into the kitchen, and surprise, it turns out to be brandy as well as coffee, or maybe Scotch, something anyway, and we go back in the living-room and sit and sip and do a lot of eye contact, and then . . . And then . . . Yes, music. I wonder if you happen to get off on Bob Marley you say in a casual sort of way, and that would be a shrewd move on your part because I do, hint, hint, and then some more eye contact, and then maybe even a bit of slow dancing it's a bit old fashioned but it's good for the old body contact and it gives us a few clues on how we might—you know.

Beam Go on.

Rose And then it's really time, no going back, eh? And I'm wondering are you the sort of chap who likes to take all my clothes off one by one very slowly or is it one each side of the bed undressing race, on your marks get set off. It's all right, you don't have to say now. Anyway, there we are, finding out who's got the coldest feet, doing our absolute level best to oblige, and then it's over, well I'm not implying as quick as all that but that is one of those things you absolutely can't predict, and anyway, we both say it was really super, even if it wasn't—but maybe—maybe it really was. (*Pause*) But, even if it really was, we still have to get up, and you have to drive me back to my car, because I do have a husband and kids at home, and I can't stay with you, Jim.

Pause

Beam Is that it, then?

Rose No, no, it's not, that's the trouble, because you can't leave it at that, can you, not civilized people like us, got to see each other again, even if it's just out of politeness, and then me being what I am, I'd stop being nervous about it and really get to like it, and we'd find out what we really like to do together, and, oh, there'd be all that smashing awful bit where I can't wait to see you, and hanging round the precinct hoping you might be doing a bit of shopping, and turning round every time a car like yours goes by, God I hope you don't drive a Cortina, and all that trying not to be the first one to say I love you, and trying not to look at my watch and trying not to notice when you do, and all that bloody compulsive *buying* you things, I'll really try not to do that too much . . . And anyway, it's double complicated with you because of all the old Primary Adviser bit and my relentless surging ambition to rise high in the Infant School Mafia, and I can get you into interviews, baby, I could make you one of the really big headmistresses, the old Puritan conscience is going to take a terrible hammering, mine too. Oh, and on and on and on, all that having to feel in the mood whenever we're together because we can't be together often and it's a shame to waste the time, so sooner or later one of us starts having to fake it now and then . . .

Beam Men can't fake it.

Rose What?

Beam Men. They can't fake it.

Rose Yes. Right! So we have all that too, what's the matter, nothing's the matter, funny never happened to me before, well really, it doesn't mean a thing, it's so pretty when it's small, all I wanted was a cuddle really, oh God is that the time, you know, all that, and then again, and the writing's on the wall, and someone has to call it a day, or do we really get down and work on it, but that's just like working on your marriage, and I've done that, rather work on the track at Chrysler. So . . . best to let it go. Say we'll always be friends and then avoid each other. I mean when you look at it, like that it hardly seems worth starting. D'you reckon? The thing is I *do* want more and I *do* want my life to change, but I don't see you and me bringing the revolution any closer, do you? Even though it seems like the only option at the moment so maybe I ought to take it. I wish you'd say something, Jim, I'm getting this awful feeling of fore- boding creeping up on me that maybe you didn't have anything like that in mind at all, maybe I'm going crackers and I can't read the signals any more, but I got so nervous I just had to say it. I'm really sorry. Spoiling your evening and that. Please say something. You've got to tell me. Was I completely up the creek?

The Lights come up very bright. Pause

Beam Only in detail. You see, I'm married too. Can't take you back. Thought we might do it in the car. It's a Maxi.

Pause

Rose (*laughing*) O.K.

The Lights fade to Black-out

Rose and Beam exit

The scene is set for Rose and Geoffrey's bedroom

Rose comes in

Rose (*softly*) Geoffrey? You asleep? Geoff?   ·

She puts the light on. He is not there

Blimey. Long meeting. Longer than mine. Can he have forgotten he's married, I ask myself.

She takes her dress off and flops down on to the chair; looks in the mirror

You look—as if you have been having—a bloody good time. Bright eyes. Pink cheeks. Mind you, it wouldn't hurt the Primary Adviser to shave twice a day. (*She smiles reflectively, then there is a pause as she lets her mind wander back to earlier in the evening. The thought of her diatribe makes her do something as extreme as banging herself on the head*) Why did I have to lay all that on him? He was just a nice man, and he thought I was interesting, and he *liked* me. And I sit there swigging his wine and going on like—and then after all that, he rallies round and gives me the most imaginative, considerate—Oh, Michael Edwardes, you don't advertise those cars the right way at all! Oh, Rose. This isn't going to bring the revolution any closer, is it? Well, yes, it *is*. In a way. Every parked car up a lane can be a blow for freedom. So to speak. No, honest, comrade. I would, I really would leave him if it wasn't for the kids. Yes, I suppose I could go and live in a women's commune. But what if they all turned out to be like Malpass and Smale? All migraines and organizing—I couldn't bloody stand it. Well yes, I could get a little house and move in with my mother and the kids. She'd love that—built-in baby-sitter, a solid base from which to sally forth as I work my way through the talent at the Council house. "Rose, you're never going out on a night like this without your vest on you?" Oh God! Sally would have us, village school, cider in the arternoons, Geoff would come and see us, practise drinking with Jake. He'd be fine with me out of the way. He doesn't want to be mucky with me any more, he wants nice clean young secretaries, sort out their critical paths, crack them from first principles. I bet he's lovely with them, he'd be fine, old Geoff, he'd cope . . . Oh, hark at her! "It's a familiar problem, Parkinson, we see a lot of it round here. To put it simply, a bottle of wine and a bit of unexpected sex drives the poor creatures barmy."

There is a sound off. She freezes

Who's that? Alex? Is that you? (*She's quite worried*) Geoffrey? Geoff, Geoff?

Geoffrey comes in in his dressing-gown. He has a bowl of something and a teaspoon

(*With relief*) Oh, it's you. I thought you were still out. I couldn't think what it was on the top floor.

Geoffrey goes and sits on the bed

What were you doing on the top floor?
Geoffrey I couldn't sleep. I went up to the playroom.
Rose What for?
Geoffrey I don't know. I was eating this.
Rose What is it?
Geoffrey (*taking a spoonful*) It's cocoa mixed up with icing sugar and tinned cream. (*He takes another spoonful*)
Rose What on earth are you eating that for?

Geoffrey Because I bloody felt like it!

She watches him scrape the bowl

I used to make this for myself when I was a kid. When my parents went out.

Rose Are you feeling all right?

Geoffrey No, I feel bloody terrible.

Rose Oh, lousy evening, was it?

Geoffrey I always have a lousy evening.

Rose You don't.

Geoffrey Where have you been tonight?

Rose A meeting. I told you.

Geoffrey You're a bloody liar.

Rose I am not a liar, I told you it was a meeting, with the Primary Adviser.

Geoffrey Then what did you take your diaphragm for?

Rose Why do you do it? You know I hate it, you know it upsets you, so why do you do it?

Geoffrey I don't know! It seemed so long waiting for you.

Rose You haven't done that for years.

Geoffrey How do you know? (*Pause*) Did you take it?

Rose Yes.

Geoffrey What for?

Rose Just in case!

Geoffrey And did you need it?

Rose Yes, as it happens. Look, stop it, I don't like this.

Geoffrey (*with his head in his hands*) Oh, Christ. (*Indistinctly into his hands*) Was it good then? Did you like it? Better than with me?

Rose Sorry? What?

Geoffrey (*shouting*) Was it good, did you like it, was it better than with me?

Rose Well, of course . . . Well, it was different, you can't compare.

Geoffrey How different?

Rose Well, it was in a car for one thing.

Long pause

Geoffrey What sort of car?

Rose A Maxi. A blue one.

Geoffrey starts to cry

Rose Geoff, oh Geoff don't, please Geoff, don't. I thought you didn't like talking about it, but you know I don't mind, so . . .

Geoffrey Can't you see how much you're hurting me?

Rose Geoffrey, that's not something I'm doing to hurt you, that's something I'm doing for myself. I'm sorry if you hurt but you're doing the hurting. (*Gently*) You are responsible for your own feelings.

Geoffrey starts to cry again

Geoffrey! This isn't fair. I thought we agreed to be reasonable, give each other a bit of freedom.

Geoffrey I can't keep it up.

Rose Oh, it's all right for you. You say you're going out for a drink or a meeting, I don't ask any questions about it, do I? I thought the idea was you'd be the same with me.

Geoffrey You want to hear what I do and who I do it with.

Rose Only if you want to tell me!

Geoffrey All right. When I say I'm going out for a drink, I go out for a drink. By myself.

Rose Jesus Christ!

Geoffrey And when I say I'm going out for a meeting, I'm going out for a drink. By myself.

Rose I don't believe you.

Geoffrey I haven't got the energy, to pull 'em any more, I haven't got the energy, I haven't the desire, haven't the need. The last one jacked me in six months ago and it was a relief, it was a bloody relief. So I sit in pubs and drink on my own. When I sense they're starting to talk about me, I change pubs, but lately I can't seem to get the pints down, and I'm home most nights by ten, wandering round the house crying, banging my head on the bathroom wall—looking through your stuff. And . . . There's this new guy at work, Targett, I was talking about him if you were listening. It's a new post. Director of personnel. Well, if he's the director of personnel, what does the personnel manager do? I can't tell what I'm supposed to do any more. I go to these meetings, and I can't understand what's going on, because all the decisions have been taken at some other meeting that I don't get invited to, and one of these days I'm going to walk into one of those meetings and it'll be well, Geoffrey, I'm sure you've been feeling as we have that you need to expand your talents in wider fields, the old chop, thank you, Geoffrey, don't come in Monday. (*He's more or less in tears again*)

Rose I didn't know, Geoff. About work.

Geoffrey You care about nothing and you notice bloody nothing!

Rose But you're good at your job, Geoff, it's just a rough patch, honest.

Geoffrey Targett took that file away from me because he didn't think I was up to it, he doesn't care what I think, I'm not even a bloody threat to him, I tell you, I wake up some mornings scared to go in.

Rose Lots of people get this.

Geoffrey I'm not lots of people.

Rose No, all right, why don't you have a word with what'shisname, you know who I mean. He could get you a month off couldn't he? Give you a chance to sort yourself—sort things out. Mm?

Geoffrey Sit round the house on my own while you're God knows where, you mean?

Rose Oh Geoff, I really did think you were having a good time.

Geoffrey You've got to give him up. You've got to stop it. I can't cope with it, Rose.

Rose Geoff, if it's that that's most important to you . . .

Geoffrey Of course it bloody is! I love you!

Rose Oh Geoffrey . . . (*She means not "I love you too, darling," but "please don't threaten me with that one"*)

Geoffrey Help me!

The Lights dim

Geoffrey and Rose exit

The bedroom set is struck, leaving the acting area bare for the following School scene. The Lights come up

Smale and Malpass enter: Malpass is in some distress

Malpass I don't think I can. When I went in there—I thought I was going to . . .

Smale You'll cope. You know I rely on you. The children need know nothing at all about it.

Malpass They'd be so upset . . .

Smale Try to relax, Beryl. Mr Stokes is in there now: he'll soon get rid of the worst of it!

Rose comes in

Rose I've just been in my classroom. Who was it?

Smale Ah, good, Mrs Fidgett, how we only have ten minutes, I'd like you to get anything you need from your room.

Rose Do you know who it was?

Smale Vandals, of course, Mrs Fidgett, but that's hardly the point.

Rose (*across this*) Well, of course it's the point!

Smale The children will be here in five minutes Mrs Fidgett.

Rose *Will you stop calling me Mrs Fidgett and listen!*

There is a shocked pause. Smale and Rose stare at each other

Malpass They took the goldfish out of the aquarium and cut them up with scissors!

Rose (*at Smale*) Kids who used to be here.

Smale There's absolutely no need to make that assumption.

Rose Well, who else would it be? Has anyone phoned the police yet?

Smale That's all been taken care of, you need not concern yourself about that.

Rose But these kids need help, we can't just ignore them.

Smale There's no need for anyone except the staff to know anything about it at all. I will speak to Mr Atkinson at the office, and nothing will get back to the parents. It's most important that this school should never be associated with anything like this. And I'll require everybody's full co-operation to ensure that. Right, off you go, Beryl.

Rose You're trying to pretend it hasn't happened, and it has! This is what they think of us! It's important!

Malpass (*in almost a wail*) My children love me!

Rose Look. Some kids must have hated so much what happened to them here that they did the worst thing they could think of, they came back and chopped up the poor old goldfish. Did we do that to them? Do we make them feel like that?

Malpass That's a disgraceful thing to say.

Smale (*on full power*) And a dangerously misguided thing to say. The trouble as I see it is that too many children are given the idea that they can think and say and do *anything they like*. And we have seen the results of that. Chopped-up goldfish and excrement on the walls! I'm sorry, Beryl!

Malpass reacts with a little weak "Oh" and runs off but Smale ignores it, really weighing into Rose

You haven't been called to any interviews, have you, Mrs Fidgett?

Rose Strong! No, I haven't.

Smale I am not at all surprised. Because before I could give you a good confidential reference, I shall expect to see a steady and continuous improvement in standards on your part, with particular reference to arithmetic, letter formation, discipline, and social training!

Smale stalks off

Pause, then Rose moves down and speaks to the audience. The Lights fade to a spot on Rose. During the following, the scene is set for Rose and Geoffrey's house

Rose Right! Hands on heads! Fingers on lips! Table six, I'm talking to you. Yes, I'm being strict. Right, hands down. Now, if any of you have got this wrong you'll be sorry. Show me your clocks. Other way up, Fraser. Now let me see the little hand pointing to the twelve. That's straight up. Point your finger to the brown wire fastened to the little hand. Now show me the big hand pointing to the three. I'm waiting, Amrik. Good. And what colour is the wire fastened to the big hand? That's right, blue. Point to the blue wire. Good. Very good, everyone. Now you all know how to leg a bomb, and you've all got one to take
. home. You're not here to ask why, Fraser, you're here to do as you're told. Now. Put your bombs carefully in your bags. Well, take your sandwich box out if there isn't any room. Good. Very good. You've all done very well. Chairs on tables! (*She stops and shakes her head as if to clear it*) Silly bugger. Might as well cut up the poor old goldfish. Smash the system. I *am* the bloody system.

Rose exits

The Lights come up. Geoffrey is at the table

(*Off*) Sarah! Alex! I'm back!

Rose enters

Oh! You're back early!

Geoffrey As you see.

Rose (*thinking—has he got the sack?*) Hey. They haven't . . .?

Geoffrey No. Not as yet. No, I was sitting at a meeting, and it suddenly occurred to me that I'd like to go home. So I got up, walked out, got in the car . . . It was easy.

Rose Think they'll—do anything about it?

Geoffrey I don't actually give a bugger about it one way or the other.

Rose Are you pissed?

Geoffrey Umm. Um—have you thought any more about what you said this morning?

Rose Just—just I still think we ought to separate.

Geoffrey Look. Um. Sit down a minute. Been thinking how to put this. Want to get it right, you see.

Rose What, Geoff?

Geoffrey Well. About half an hour after I got home, Sarah came back from Cindy's.

Rose *(alarmed for Sarah)* What's the matter?

Geoffrey Nothing's the matter with her. That's not it. Well, she sat down here with me and started telling me how things had gone at Cindy's, and the various odd ways of the Cindy household—and then she branched off into the good and bad points of some of her other friends—and what might make her flute teacher so sarcastic . . .

Rose What's all this about?

Geoffrey D'you think you could just listen please? Anyway. It seemed as if what she wanted was a really good long chat. So I got a bottle out—and I sat here drinking and listening, and she sat—on the table here, telling me all her stuff. Sitting on the table, with her feet resting on my knees.

There is a long pause. Rose wonders what the hell is this going to lead up to? What frightful revelation? He seems so intent

Rose Look . . .

Geoffrey That was all, you see. Except that—actually while it was going on, not bloody afterwards, or when it was too late, I was thinking that there was absolutely nothing that I'd rather be doing than what I was doing, and absolutely no-one I'd rather be with than the person I was with. D'you see what I mean?

Rose Yes.

Geoffrey I don't know about you, but that's a bloody rare feeling for me. *(Pause)* If—when you leave me, who did you reckon was going to have the kids?

Rose Well, I would, of course. That's what I thought. Didn't you? I'd manage, people do.

Geoffrey Could you manage without them?

Rose No.

Geoffrey Yeah. Thought I ought to mention it. You see, I'd fight you for them, Rose. And, courts being what they are, the odds are that you'd get them. I thought I ought to tell you that if you take the kids away from me I'll kill myself.

Pause

Rose I don't believe you.

Geoffrey That's up to you.

Rose You wouldn't. You're just . . . You bastard, Geoff, I won't have that laid on me!

Geoffrey I'm not laying anything on you, you stupid bitch. I'm simply telling you the way things are, and what you do about them is up to you.

Child (*off*) Dad!

Geoffrey Excuse me.

Geoffrey gets up and goes out

The Lights dim and the voices of children are heard singing. The house set is struck, leaving the acting area bare

Voices (*off; singing*) All things bright and beautiful
                           All creatures great and small
                           All things wise and wonderful
                           The Lord God made them all.

Rose comes forward and the Lights come up and concentrate on her

Rose O.K. Class Three, gather round. Come on, dinosaurs, let's see your faces. Thank you. Now what day is it today? Rachel? Wednesday, right. And who's going to do the calendar today? All right, Fraser, thank you very much. Now, who's noticed anything new today? Yes. New paint on the walls. Like it? Same as before only cleaner, right. They can't fool you, eh Jason? Anything else? No, the goldfish haven't come back. Well, they can't, Rachel, because they're dead, but I've got us two new ones. And we'll have to think up some good names for them. And how we're going to look after them. That's right, Amrik. They can't look after themselves like we can. We're in charge, right? Because listen. When you're grown up, you are going to have to make up your own minds about things. There won't always be a teacher there. And for that, you have to practise. Right? O.K. then. So, what are we going to do today?

CURTAIN

FURNITURE AND PROPERTY LIST

ACT I

On stage: SLOPS WINE BAR:
Small table. *On it:* half-pint of bitter, glass of sherry, 2 beer mats
Hatstand. *On it:* Slate with prices of various drinks

Off stage: ASSEMBLY:
Piano stool
Upright piano
2 small chairs

STAFF ROOM:
2 upright armchairs
1 small chair
Filing cabinet. *On it:* electric kettle (practical), jar of instant coffee,
3 mugs, milk bottle, 3 spoons, sugar bowl

SCHOOLROOM:
Teacher's desk. *On it:* various books, papers, pens, jar of paintbrushes
rulers, general dressing

SALLYS FLAT
Large two-piece sofa
Low bookcase-table. *On shelf:* books
Rug. *On it:* pile of magazines

ROSE AND GEOFFREY'S HOUSE:
Kitchen-type table. *On it:* papers, pen
4 small chairs
1 wooden armchair
Waste-bin

All the above are set by Stage Management during the action

File, papers, pen **(Smale)**
File. *In it:* drawing of dog **(Malpass)**
Large, shabby attaché case **(Rose)**
Copy of *The Guardian* **(Rose)**

Personal: **Mother:** handbag with pound note, wristwatch
Beam: spectacles
Sally: spectacles
Malpass: lipstick

ACT II

On stage: Double bed. *On it:* **Rose**'s dress, cigarettes and lighter
Bed-table
Dressing-table. *On it:* various articles of make-up
Small chair

Off stage: WINE BAR (alterations from Act I)
On table: empty wine bottle, 2 wine glasses

ROSE AND GEOFFREY'S HOUSE (alterations from Act I)
On table: half-empty wine bottle, glass
Full wine bottle **(Beam)**
Bowl of "mixture", teaspoon **(Geoffrey)**

Personal: **Geoffrey:** comb

EFFECTS PLOT

ACT I

Cue 1   **Jake:** "No, Rose."   (Page 1)
Sound of children's voices

Cue 2   **Geoffrey:** ". . . you notice bloody nothing."   (Page 1)
Increase volume of voices

Cue 3   **Smale:** "That's better."   (Page 1)
Fade voices

ACT II

Cue 4   **Father:** "You dirty little bugger."   (Page 30)
Sound of a slap

Cue 5   **Rose** switches off lights   (Page 34)
Wine bar music—fade as dialogue starts

Cue 6   **Geoffrey** goes out   (Page 44)
Sound of children singing "All Things Bright And Beautiful"

LIGHTING PLOT

Property fittings required: nil
Various simple interior sets on an open stage

ACT I

To open: Spot on Rose at table. Off-stage lights behind doors as they open

Cue 1	As opening chorus of voices finishes *Snap off off-stage lights, bring up acting area lights to full*	(Page 1)
Cue 2	**Smale** smoothes the shaking **Malpass** *The lights fade to about ½ and then light up on* **Rose**	(Page 13)
Cue 3	**Rose:** ". . . and the Primary Adviser." *Return to full lighting*	(Page 13)
Cue 4	**Geoffrey** exits *Fade to spot on* **Rose**	(Page 24)
Cue 5	**Rose:** ". . . all in it together." *Return to full lighting* .	(page 25)
Cue 6	**Malpass** exits *Concentrate lighting on* **Rose**	(Page 27)
Cue 7	**Rose:** ". . . talking to someone, that's all." *Bring up off-stage doors lighting as characters speak, as opening of Act*	(Page 27)
Cue 8	**Rose:** "Fine." *Fade to Black-out*	(Page 27)

ACT II

To open: Full lighting on acting area

Cue 9	**Mother:** ". . . what I mean, Rose." **Rose:** "Yes." *Concentrate lighting on* **Rose**	(Page 30)
Cue 10	The sound of a slap *Return to full lighting*	(Page 30)
Cue 11	**Rose** switches off lights *Black-out*	(Page 34)
Cue 12	As Wine Bar music starts *Fade up very slowly to concentration on table*	(Page 34)

Lightning Source UK Ltd.
Milton Keynes UK
UKOW05f1930111216
289692UK00001B/46/P